WORLD'S CUTEST ANIMALS

WORLD'S CUTEST ANIMALS

Copyright © Summersdale Publishers, 2012

With research by Anna Martin

Summersdale Publishers Ltd
46 West Street
Chichester
West Sussex
PO19 1RP
UK

www.summersdale.com

Printed and bound in China

ISBN: 978-1-84953-304-1

Substantial discounts on bulk quantities of Summersdale books are available to corporations, professional associations and other organisations. For details contact Summersdale Publishers by telephone: +44 (0) 1243 771107, fax: +44 (0) 1243 786300 or email: nicky@summersdale.com.

WORLD'S CUTEST ANIMALS

JOSIE RIPLEY

summersdale

CONTENTS

INTRODUCTION

The animal world contains more cuddly cuteness than a toyshop window: there are classic furry lovelies like the chubby, teddy-bear-like koala, the smiley, sleepy-eyed sloth and the Dumbo-eared fennec fox; but within this book you will discover that all manner of curious critters – scaly, feathered and fuzzy – have a serious 'ahhhh' factor, and some astonishing qualities that might just make you go, 'Wow!' This book has everything, from the tiny, jewel-like hummingbird, the only bird with the aerobatic skills to fly upside down and backwards, to the colourful clownfish, which can live in harmony with stinging anemones and has the ability to change from male to female – that never happened in *Finding Nemo*!

Read on and prepare to be captivated by the snuggliest, cutest, sweetest creatures on the planet, each with their own 'cutest feature' detail and one- to five-star 'snuggle rating'. Whether you're tickled by fuzzy tree-dwellers with saucer-sized eyes, blow-up fish or scaly but loveable beasts small enough to perch on the tip of your finger, there is something here for everyone!

FENNEC FOX

Vulpes zerda

LIVES Deserts of North Africa and the Sinai and Arabian peninsulas

EATS Small rodents, reptiles, plants, insects

The fennec fox is the smallest member of the fox family, ranging from 24–40 cm in length, with a big, bushy tail which can be up to 20 cm long. It is obviously blessed in the ear department, but its Dumbo-sized flappers are not just for show: they are filled with blood vessels close to the surface of the skin, which helps the fox release body heat to dissipate the extreme temperatures of the deserts in which it resides. The fox also boasts a copious covering of fuzzy fur on the soles of its feet, which acts like slippers protecting it from the searing heat of the dunes. The fennec is nocturnal, but it does like to sunbathe.

The fennec is quite a sociable animal, choosing to live in a small pack, and in parts of North America and North Africa they are kept as pets, much like cats and dogs – they even purr like cats when happy. The French aviator and author Antoine de Saint-Exupéry had a fennec as a pet and it is believed that his furry friend inspired the fox character in his book *The Little Prince*.

CUTEST FEATURE: Those ears!

SNUGGLE RATING: ****

SEAHORSE

Hippocampus (family)
LIVES Tropical or temperate seas
EATS Tiny fish, plankton, shrimp

Despite being commonly known as the 'stallion of the sea', this other-worldly creature is a surprisingly poor swimmer, and for that reason it is almost always resting, wrapping its prehensile tail around a stationary object such as a plant frond. The seahorse swims upright, using the pectoral fins behind its ears to steer, and has coronets atop its horsey head which gives it an almost regal appearance.

It uses its extra-long snout to slurp up plankton and tiny fish, but because the seahorse doesn't have teeth or a stomach food passes through its insides incredibly quickly, which means it has to eat constantly to stay alive.

This tiny creature has an unusual courtship and mating ritual, and in tropical seas the mating season lasts all year! The female seahorse will deposit her eggs into the male's pouch where they are fertilised and carried until the babies are ready to emerge two to four weeks later – yes, it's the male that becomes pregnant and gives birth! The number of babies born in one birth can be as few as five or as many as 1,500.

CUTEST FEATURE: Their horsey faces and long snouts
SNUGGLE RATING: ** (Well, they are wet fish!)

FALLOW DEER

Dama dama

LIVES Woodland, scrubland, meadows and parks throughout Western and Central Europe

EATS Grasses, brambles, leaves, fruits, bark, nuts, fungi

This graceful-looking creature has the most beautiful Bambi-like white speckled coat, which can vary from white to chestnut-brown to red to black, depending on the time of year. It also has a fetching black streak along its spine, like a go-faster stripe, that extends to the tip of its white tail.

With its powerful, lean frame the fallow deer can reach speeds of up to 30 mph and can jump an amazing 5 m high. Fallow deer were introduced to Europe in the eleventh century by the Romans and are a mainstay of parkland, especially the royal parks throughout the UK. It roams in single sex herds for much of the year, choosing to mate once a year in the autumn in what is known as the 'rutting season', which can be a noisy affair in which the males will bark and lock horns to fend off rivals – the barking sounds not unlike belching!

CUTEST FEATURE: Its doe eyes and the spring in its step
SNUGGLE RATING: ***

DUGONG

Dugong dugon
LIVES Indo-Pacific region, but mostly in Shark Bay off northern Australia
EATS Seagrass, small shellfish

This prehistoric-looking, gentle giant of the sea is more commonly known as the 'sea cow' because it spends its days grazing on seagrass in shallow waters. It is not like any other marine animal and is most closely related to the elephant! The dugong can grow to a maximum length of 3 m and weigh up to half a tonne, which explains why it lives life in the slow lane.

Because of its slow pace the dugong has many predators, including humans who hunt it for oil and meat, and numbers have declined sharply over the centuries – where once the sea cow could survive in large herds, it is now more likely to see just one or two dugongs together. As a result, this timid creature is now regarded as a protected species in Australia.

The dugong's other-worldly appearance and graceful actions in the water are believed to have inspired the legend of mermaids.

CUTEST FEATURE: Its sweet face, with its friendly eyes and protruding, snuffling nose
SNUGGLE RATING: **

RED PANDA

Ailurus fulgens

LIVES Mountain regions of Nepal, India, Laos, Bhutan, Myanmar and central China

EATS Bamboo, fruits, acorns, leaves, eggs

This compact, cuddly-looking creature with its bold, ringed tail bears little resemblance to its distant relative the giant panda – the red panda grows to about the size of a domestic cat and looks not unlike a raccoon, also a distant genetic relative. The two bears do, however, share the same rainy, high-altitude habitat, but the red panda, with its strong claws perfectly adapted to climbing, prefers to dwell amongst the treetops rather than the forest floor and spends much of the day curled up in a tree with its tail wrapped around its head.

Its distinctive thick, fur coat protects it from the cold and wet – it even has fur on its paw pads to help it to grip on to the wet bark and leaves – and, although vibrant in colour, the redness of its coat acts as camouflage against the red moss found in its habitat. Interestingly, the red panda is sometimes referred to as the 'firefox' and the collective noun for these beautiful beasts is a 'sleuth'.

CUTEST FEATURE: Its fluffy ringed tail
SNUGGLE RATING: ★★★★

HUMMINGBIRD

Trochilidae (family)
LIVES Central and South America
EATS Nectar, small insects

Early Spanish explorers of the New World called the hummingbird a 'flying jewel' and it's easy to see why. You need sharp eyesight to spot this exotic-coloured bird, because it zips from flower to flower at up to 35 mph, reaching speeds of 60 mph when diving through the air for gnats and other tiny, unsuspecting insects.

The hummingbird beats its wings up to an astonishing 80 times a second, and it's tiny – not growing to more than 7–9 cm. It is also the only bird that can fly backwards, up, down, upside down (for short periods) or appear to hover in mid-air. The 'hum' of the hummingbird is created by the sound of its ferociously fast wings, and its long, sword-shaped bill enables it to reach the nectar in a flower's corolla.

Unbelievably, the tiny hummingbird migrates: the ruby-throat, for example, will make the 2,000-mile journey from Canada to Panama, which includes an impressive non-stop 500-mile stretch across the Gulf of Mexico.

CUTEST FEATURE: Its beautiful colours and zippiness
SNUGGLE RATING: **

EUROPEAN PINE MARTEN

Martes martes

LIVES Woodlands throughout central and northern Europe

EATS Nuts, berries, birds' eggs, small mammals, including grey squirrels

This diminutive and elusive forest-dweller is a member of the weasel family and it's not hard to see the family resemblance, with its long, sleek body, equally long tail, sweet, proud head with rounded ears, dark eyes and tickly whiskers. The pine marten is about the size of a domestic cat and is often dark brown with a creamy coloured 'bib' on its throat. It is mainly nocturnal, and with its clever retractable claws it can make light work of scaling tall trees as well as scampering at great speeds along the forest floor.

The pine marten tends to set up home in tree hollows, but this little devil has been known to live rent-free in lofts and outbuildings. It's more likely that you would see evidence of a pine marten, such as footprints or droppings, than the creature itself, but they are curious and will inspect the goodies on a bird table as well as sidle up to lighted windows to peer inside.

CUTEST FEATURE: Its curious nature

SNUGGLE RATING: ***

CUTE
ANIMAL FACTS

Squirrels are known for being great hoarders of seed and nuts, but they can also be a little forgetful as to where they have hidden their treasure. As a happy consequence millions of trees are planted accidentally by these furry tree-dwellers each year! A squirrel is very guarded about its nuts and it will even make elaborate displays of burying non-existent nuts and seeds to throw its rivals off the scent.

One of the most bizarre animal adoption stories ever involves the pairing of a 130-year-old male giant tortoise and a baby hippopotamus. The hippo lost its mother during the Boxing Day tsunami in 2004 and was rescued by wildlife rangers on the Kenyan coast. It soon struck up a close bond with an old tortoise, which took on a maternal, nurturing role to the baby hippo, resulting in the pair eating, playing and snoozing together.

GOLDEN LION TAMARIN

Leontopithecus rosalia
LIVES Atlantic coastal forests in Brazil
EATS Fruits, berries, insects

This golden-orange monkey with its impressive lion-like mane and charismatic face inhabits canopied rainforests in Brazil. The forests in which it lives provide a rich source of fruits and insects for the tamarin to eat and the canopy provides protection from airborne predators, such as hawks. When the tamarin spots a predator it will make a distinctive call to its troop (between two and nine other monkeys) and head for hollows in tree trunks to hide, or, if there is nowhere to hide, it will drop to the forest floor.

The tamarin is a very social creature; it will share food that it has foraged, participate in mutual grooming sessions and even the male monkeys will do their fair share of rearing the young. A tamarin troop will defend its territory from other troops by marking its patch of forest with scent and calling from the trees – it never leads to physical altercations though, just a bit of monkeying around. In the wild a tamarin will live for an average eight years, but one tamarin living in captivity in a Texan zoo lived to 31 years old!

CUTEST FEATURE: Its lion-like mane
SNUGGLE RATING: ★★★★

GLASS FROG

Centrolenidae anura
LIVES Cloud forests of Central and South America
EATS Small insects, fish, other frogs

This highly unusual member of the tree frog family has partially transparent skin, allowing its fragile bones and red veins to be seen clearly. The glass frog's glossy, leaf-green skin, diminutive size (not more than 3 cm) and gold-framed eyes make it look like a tiny, beautiful jade ornament, and as a result it is perfectly camouflaged among the lush leaves of the rainforest. During the breeding season it will lay its eggs on leaves overhanging fast-flowing rivers, allowing the hatched tadpoles to drop into the water.

This fragile creature is happiest foraging at night in light rain which keeps its skin moist, however, it will take cover in heavy showers as it can be killed by the impact of a single raindrop. The male glass frog is territorial and will challenge an invading male to a wrestling match which will only finish when one opponent is pinned to the floor, before hopping back to where he came from.

CUTEST FEATURE: Its gold-ringed eyes
SNUGGLE RATING: **

SLOW LORIS

Lorisidae (family)
LIVES Rainforests in South East Asia
EATS Tree gum, fruits, insects, small mammals

This furry, big-eyed fellow may look impossibly cute, but don't be fooled because it's not altogether friendly. It happens to be the world's most venomous primate, packing some serious ammo in its elbows, of all places.

Sadly, this nocturnal, slow-moving tree-dweller is a victim of illegal pet trading – its teeth are removed to make it safe – and it is highly prized for its supposed medicinal and supernatural properties. Some people believe that the loris can ward off evil spirits and accelerate the healing of wounds and illness, and around three centuries ago, natives of Borneo believed that it was a gatekeeper to the afterlife.

It is a sitting duck to its enemies, as it chooses to amble around in a sleepy fashion, much like the sloth, rather than run for cover at the first sign of danger. Its pincer-like hands and feet make it perfectly adapted to life among the treetops, where its saucer-sized eyes help it to forage for food in the dark.

CUTEST FEATURE: The constant surprised look on its little face
SNUGGLE RATING: ***

BOTTLENOSE DOLPHIN

Tursiops truncates
LIVES Coastal waters of the Atlantic
EATS All types of fish

The stunning bottlenose dolphin is so-called because its nose is, unsurprisingly, bottle-shaped, and it always looks as if it has a smile on its face due to the way its mouth curves.

This cheeky marine mammal is a veritable aquatic acrobat and can jump up to 6 m above the water, and it is a friendly fellow (or maybe just a little bit nosy!), as it will often swim up to people or alongside boats and allow its silky-smooth skin to be stroked.

Listening to one of these beauties is like attending a rock concert, with all of the shrill squeaks, groans and whistles – it's the dolphin's nasal sacs inside its head which allow it to 'talk' – and each dolphin has a unique whistle, though it would be impossible for a human to discern them. The bottlenose makes clicking noises in the water, up to a thousand clicks per second, to locate objects, using the sound waves which bounce off an object and echo back to it, revealing its relative distance and position. It lives in pods of up to twelve dolphins and is without doubt the cleverest thing with a dorsal fin!

CUTEST FEATURE: Its permanent grin and friendliness to other animals and humans

SNUGGLE RATING: ★★★★

AFRICAN PYGMY
HEDGEHOG

Atelerix albiventris

LIVES Central and eastern Africa; a house near you when kept as a domestic pet!

EATS Mealworms, insects, grubs, quality cat food

This unusual, prickly little creature is a cross between the Algerian hedgehog and the white-bellied four-toed hedgehog and with its magnificent mullet of white spikes it looks like something out of the 1980s. This particular breed has become popular as a domestic pet in recent years.

The domestic pygmy hedgehog's wild counterparts are great walkers, travelling for miles at night in the woods, swamps and grasslands of Africa searching for tasty morsels, as well as climbing and swimming when the need arises. A house-kept hedgehog will prefer to pound the treadmill and feast on mealworms or quality cat treats while everyone sleeps. It is quite a tough little critter, being able to consume poisonous scorpions and even snakes! When threatened by a predator it will let out a shrill scream and simply curl into a prickly, mace-like ball, which isn't very appetising at all!

CUTEST FEATURE: Its spiky hairdo

SNUGGLE RATING: **

TAMANDUA

Tamandua tetradactyla
LIVES Mexico, Central and South America
EATS Beetles, bees, insects, fruits, occasionally meat

The tamandua is a type of anteater, but it is much smaller than its anteater relatives, growing to a maximum of 90 cm. It has a rather unappealing nickname – 'the stinker of the forest' – because of its rather pungent odour; you wouldn't want to be in the line of fire of one of these little critters, because they can emit a whiff that's four times more potent than a skunk's! It also has tremendous claws, which it uses to swipe at anything that's threatening it.

But, despite these less friendly characteristics, the tamandua is rather cute with its long, beaky nose, tiny eyes and curly tail. It has a voracious appetite, slurping up as many as 9,000 ants in a single day with its 40-cm-long sticky tongue. It also enjoys honey and bees direct from the beehive.

This curious animal is most active at night and tends to be solitary; it has poor eyesight but a keen sense of smell and hearing, and likes to sleep in the day, with its fluffy tail acting as a pillow.

CUTEST FEATURE: Its long snout and beady eyes
SNUGGLE RATING: ***

GOLDCREST

Regulus regulus
LIVES UK and Scandinavia
EATS Small insects

The whimsical goldcrest is the most petite bird to be found in Europe, being only 8–9 cm long and with a wingspan of just 14–15 cm. It has golden crest feathers and a rather fetching olive-green plumage with black and white striped wings.

What this tiny bird lacks in size it makes up for in ingenuity, making its nest out of delicate spiders' webs and moss on slender branches in conifer trees and ivy. The female goldcrest lays pale eggs with brown speckles and both parents feed the young once hatched.

The goldcrest has earned the impressive title of 'the king of birds' in European folklore after, according to Aristotle and Pliny the Elder, it won a contest amongst the birds to see who could fly the highest. The eagle was the favourite to win, but as it grew tired of soaring ever upward, a tiny bird that had been hiding under the eagle's wing – our goldcrest – emerged, flying above the eagle to claim the title.

CUTEST FEATURE: Its tiny frame
SNUGGLE RATING: **

CUTE ANIMAL FACTS

Did you know that the giant panda bleats like a goat? It doesn't growl or roar like a grizzly bear, choosing to communicate with friendly little baaing and honking sounds. It can sneeze, too, when its nose gets a tickle, just like you and me.

The koala wins the award for the world's sleepiest animal, sometimes clocking up 22 hours of napping per day! The brown bat and the sloth come in at a close second, sleeping 20 hours a day. This is in stark contrast to other animals such as the giraffe which can manage on a few minutes' sleep, and whales and dolphins that don't sleep a wink for their first year of life.

OTTER

Lutrinae (family)
LIVES UK, India, China, Africa, Asia, Europe, Russia
EATS Shellfish, small fish, amphibians, birds, mammals

This intelligent, semi-aquatic creature is among the most playful of the water mammals. It appears to enjoy lunging down muddy banks and snowy hills, as well as taking delight in chasing and hunting down small waterborne creatures in packs.

The otter is particularly adept at breaking open shellfish, such as mussels and clams, which it does by finding a pebble and hitting the shell with it, using its belly as a butcher's block. It has a long, slim body, short arms and webbed feet, which enable it to glide through water as well as negotiate riverbanks and wetlands with ease. Its soft fur traps air bubbles, giving it a magical, silvery appearance which also insulates it from the cold and keeps it dry.

The otter's rounded head could have easily been designed by a cuddly toy maker, with its button black nose and exquisite fuzzy face. There are 13 species of otter; some are freshwater dwellers and some live in seas – all are cute!

CUTEST FEATURE: Its playful nature
SNUGGLE RATING: ****

SQUIRREL MONKEY

Saimiri sciureus

LIVES Tropical rainforests, mangroves and marshlands of South America

EATS Insects, small vertebrates, eggs, fruits

This olive-coloured cheeky monkey is known to live in large groups, ranging from 20 or so to as many as 500 in undisturbed areas of rainforest. It prefers to live in the middle canopy but will also venture to the treetops and forest floor in its search for tasty morsels, which can include tree frogs and birds' eggs.

With its black mouth and white brows and ears, it has earned the nickname of the 'death's head monkey', but there's nothing sinister about this cutie pie. In fact, this kind of monkey has proven popular as a domestic pet, particularly in the US, and has even been involved in matters of great national importance: 26 squirrel monkeys were once purchased from a pet shop in Florida to take part in America's quest to win the space race. One monkey in particular, known as Miss Baker, achieved global recognition when she was launched into space in 1959 in a shoebox-sized capsule. She wore a tiny space helmet and jacket for her out-of-this-world encounter, orbiting for 16 minutes before returning to Earth unharmed.

CUTEST FEATURE: Being out of this world!

SNUGGLE RATING: ***

SUGAR GLIDER

Petaurus breviceps
LIVES Australia, New Guinea, Indonesia
EATS Eucalyptus sap, nectar, insects

Despite having a name that wouldn't be out of place on a reality show, there's nothing shabby about this gorgeous little marsupial. The sugar glider can float through the air, much like the flying squirrel, thanks to a membrane that extends along its body, from its fifth finger to its first toe. When its legs are fully outstretched, it can glide for a maximum of 150 m from tree to tree as it hunts for insects, vertebrates and sap from trees such as acacia and eucalyptus.

Being nocturnal it has huge eyes, big ears for hearing and a long snout for smelling. The glider is a popular pet in parts of America and thrives in a warm home; it loves to be handled or kept warm in a coat pocket. In the wild it will sleep for much of the day, up to 22 hours, to conserve its energy. It has unusually placed scent glands, one on its forehead, another on its chest and another on its cloaca (an opening near its tail end), which it uses to mark its territory and to scent its mates. It can reach a maximum size of 30 cm, from its nose to the tip of its prehensile tail.

CUTEST FEATURE: Its ability to fly
SNUGGLE RATING: ****

ANGORA RABBIT

Oryctolagus cuniculus
LIVES As a domestic pet in many a home
EATS Seeds, vegetables

This big, soft, powder puff of an animal looks like it belongs on a dressing table rather than in a hutch! It's so fluffy that it looks like a cloud or perhaps a snowball with ears. The angora rabbit needs an awful lot of grooming due to its enormous bouffant-like fur, and requires a regular brush and cool blow-dry to keep it looking at its fuzzy best. However, its fur is more than just for show: the hair, which moults every four months or so, can be removed by shearing, plucking or combing to be made into wool for garments such as scarves and jumpers.

The angora rabbit was discovered in the Turkish port of Angora (now Ankara) in the sixteenth century and exported to France and other parts of Europe to be farmed for its wool. It was a popular pet among French royalty in the eighteenth century, and it is considered to be the perfect house pet, being docile, curious and receptive to plenty of cuddles, stroking and grooming, and it lives to an impressive seven years of age.

CUTEST FEATURE: Its outrageous fluffy fur
SNUGGLE RATING: *****

CHAMELEON

Chamaeleonidae (family)

LIVES Sub-Saharan Africa, Madagascar, northern Africa, southern Europe, Middle East, India, Sri Lanka

EATS Insects, other lizards, small birds, leaves, berries

This ancient-looking creature has 160 varieties, ranging in size from a teeny tiny 1.5 cm long up to a whopping 70 cm, and some even have dinosaur-esque horns on their heads.

The chameleon has the superior ability of being able to change colour to reflect its mood: for example, it will turn red or yellow when spoiling for a fight, or to its flashiest colours when trying to attract a mate, and will adopt a default colour to blend in with its environment.

The chameleon has many other wonderfully weird skills: it can whip its long tongue out so quickly that it can't be followed by the human eye, and its swivelling, stereoscopic eyes can work independently to enable it to see two different things at once. It has specially adapted feet for climbing; the five toes on each foot are fused together into a group of two and three, giving them a mitten-like appearance.

CUTEST FEATURE: You can tell its mood by the colour of its skin!
SNUGGLE RATING: **

48

SLOTH

Bradypodidae or Megalonychidae (family)
LIVES Jungles of Central and South America
EATS Leaves, shoots, fruits

The sloth is officially the slowest animal in the world; in fact, it's so slow that even algae grows on it, as if it were a tree. It sleeps up to 20 hours a day, hanging from branches with its incredible razor-sharp claws.

As the sloth is so docile, it has the appearance of being permanently happy and chilled out, with its upturned mouth and gleaming black eyes, and black rings around its eyes like a Zorro mask that just make you want to go, 'Ahhhh!' To compensate for its lack of mobility, the sloth has a head that it can swivel around 270 degrees, thus further eliminating the need to move more than is absolutely necessary to survey its surroundings.

This lazy bones even mates and gives birth while hanging from trees, and its babies cling on to their mother for nine months before venturing off to a branch of their own. Surprisingly, sloths are competent swimmers as they have strong forearms enabling them to power through the water.

CUTEST FEATURE: The mask of Zorro!
SNUGGLE RATING: ***

MEERKAT

Suricata suricatta

LIVES Deserts of South Africa, Namibia and Botswana

EATS Insects, scorpions, spiders, small mammals, plants, eggs

This comical creature always looks like it is up to mischief as it stands on its hind legs and peers around for predators. It has dark markings round its eyes, which act like sunglasses as it sunbathes in the dazzlingly bright desert sun.

The meerkat lives in 'gangs' of up to 50, making its home in extensive underground burrows with many entrances; they even share a communal toilet! One or two meerkats will stand sentry-like on their hind legs, barking if there is danger nearby or making different calls depending on the location and type of predator, while others will forage for food for the colony.

The meerkat is an incredibly hospitable little critter and will even accommodate other animals in its burrow, including ground squirrels and yellow mongooses. Occasionally, snakes will find their way in, which is bad news as snakes see meerkats as prey. Every meerkat loves to play: some have even been observed wrestling and racing each other!

CUTEST FEATURE: Its nosiness!

SNUGGLE RATING: ✴✴✴✴

CLOWNFISH

Amphiprion percula
LIVES Reefs in the Pacific and Indian Oceans, Red Sea
EATS Algae, plankton, small molluscs, crustaceans

The clownfish, or false anemone fish to give it its proper name, is one of the world's most widely recognised fish, thanks to a Disney film called *Finding Nemo*. This handsome fellow is bright orange with three distinctive white vertical stripes on its body, and can grow to around 11 cm in length.

It lives among the reefs in tropical waters and makes its home among anemones. Anemones can be lethal to other fish, as they emit a poisonous sting, but the clownfish has a protective layer of mucus on its skin which makes it immune. In return for the anemone playing host and protecting the clownfish, the fish will nibble away any parasites and preen the anemone, like performing a regular spring clean.

Each and every clownfish is born male and can change to female, but only once as the process is irreversible. When two male clownfish pair up, one will become female so that they can reproduce, and when the female dies another male will change gender to take its place!

CUTEST FEATURE: Its colourful stripes
SNUGGLE RATING: **

CUTE ANIMAL FACTS

Jeff Daniel from Wigan must have the most unusual cycling partner ever: whereas some might take the family pooch for a brisk stroll or a cycle, he has a pet racing pigeon to accompany him. He nurtured the bird from when it was a month old and the pigeon, called Prince, considers Jeff as his parent, loyally and rather sweetly following him wherever he goes.

It's a well-known fact that pigs can't fly, but what about goats? In Morocco one farmer was greeted with the most extraordinary sight – his favourite billies had climbed to the highest branches of a tree and appeared like birds, perched up high. And why was this? Well, due to the dry conditions and lack of sustenance the bleaters took matters into their own hands to retrieve the few mouthfuls of the argan tree's berries, spreading out their two-toed feet to grip the trunk and shin up to the goodies.

KOALA

Phascolarctos cinereus
LIVES Australia
EATS Eucalyptus leaves

The koala is the living embodiment of the teddy bear: with its rounded head and plump body, stubby arms, rounded ears, small, beady eyes, big black leathery nose and thick fuzzy fur it is the epitome of cute. But despite appearances it is not actually a bear, but rather a marsupial.

The koala is a solitary animal – each has its own tree, which is not visited by other koalas apart from during the mating season. Like other marsupials, such as kangaroos, a mother koala will carry its baby in a pouch until it is big enough to ride on her back or tummy. An adult koala is slow-moving and will spend around 18 hours asleep each day, and because it spends so long nestled in the crooks of trees it has developed an inbuilt cushion on its bottom for added comfort.

The word 'koala' is believed to derive from an Aboriginal word meaning 'no drink', because a koala obtains most of its moisture from leaves, and with its penchant for eucalyptus it tends to have the lingering smell of herbal cough drops.

CUTEST FEATURE: Its cuddly teddy bear body
SNUGGLE RATING: *****

PENGUIN

Spheniscidae (family)
LIVES Southern hemisphere, predominantly Antarctica
EATS Krill, squid, fish

This bird is the Charlie Chaplin of the animal world, with its distinctive waddle and black and white markings like an old-fashioned tuxedo. There are around 20 different species of penguin and although it may look decidedly awkward on land, choosing to either walk on its flippers or 'toboggan' on its stomach, with the further disadvantage of being flightless, once it hits the water its flippers and aerodynamic body transforms it into a highly efficient swimmer.

The diving penguin can reach depths of over half a kilometre and stay underwater for up to 22 minutes! Because the penguin has no land predators, it is seemingly unafraid of humans and will walk straight up to them. Amazingly, archaeologists have found remains of prehistoric penguins that were the size and weight of an adult human – just imagine!

CUTEST FEATURE: Its waddle
SNUGGLE RATING: ****

PYGMY MARMOSET

Cebuella pygmaea
LIVES Rainforests in South America
EATS Tree sap and gum, berries, insects

The pygmy marmoset, or 'finger-monkey', is the smallest monkey in the world. Incredibly, its body is often no longer than the average adult human finger and it rarely weighs much more than an apple.

This teeny tike has a distinctive ringed tail and tawny green-coloured fur and, being so small, is a tasty morsel for birds of prey. However, these little creatures can move swiftly, and are able to jump up to 5 m, climbing very high on slender branches. The marmoset communicates by making a series of bird-like squeaks and pips – some shrieks are so high-pitched that humans can't hear them. Because of its diminutive appearance, and being the cutest monkey in the animal kingdom, it is a popular pet, particularly in North America, but it does have some antisocial habits, such as flicking poo and biting when threatened. In the wild, it is a gentle, docile creature, enjoying social bonding like mutual grooming within its family group of up to nine monkeys.

CUTEST FEATURE: It's finger-sized – the tiniest, cutest monkey in the world!
SNUGGLE RATING: *****

PIKA

Ochotona princeps

LIVES Rocky mountainsides and alpine meadows with cold climates in Asia, North America and Eastern Europe

EATS Leaves, grasses, seeds, weeds, berries

The pika is one of the smallest members of the rabbit family: although it looks more like a mouse with its brown, furry egg-shaped body, long whiskers and small, rounded ears rather than the usual bunny flappers, like its rabbit relatives it doesn't have a tail. It is a shy creature, but it can often be heard whistling to other pikas out in open rocky areas.

The pint-sized pika gathers flowers and grasses throughout the warmer months, sun-drying them in preparation for winter – it can make a hay store the size of a haystack, in which it buries its food supplies. The pika lives in colonies and has its own territories that it actively defends by marking its territory and making alarm calls. It lives up to seven years in the wild or captivity.

CUTEST FEATURE: The way it whistles to its friends

SNUGGLE RATING: ***

LADYBIRD

Coccinellidae (family)
LIVES Worldwide
EATS Greenfly, small insects, vegetation

This beautiful insect that almost looks hand-painted is also known as a ladybug, lady fly, God's cow and even lady cow! It has a dome-shaped, oval body and comes in a dazzling array of bright Smartie-like colours, with mainly black spots or stripes or, sometimes, no markings at all.

The ladybird is the saviour of many gardens, as it can munch its way through as many as 5,000 aphids in a lifetime, and many cultures consider ladybirds to be symbols of good luck. Its bright colours spell danger to other creatures and serve as a warning that they are poisonous when eaten, but this insect is completely harmless to humans. It is a winged insect, and in flight it beats its wings up to 85 times a second.

CUTEST FEATURE: Its beautiful colours
SNUGGLE RATING: **

MATSCHIE'S TREE-KANGAROO

Dendrolagus matschiei
LIVES Tropical forests in Indonesia, Papua New Guinea and Australia
EATS Leaves, fruits, flowers, sap, eggs, grains

These golden and chestnut-brown, long-lashed lovelies are the prettier cousin to the better-known kangaroo. Being a tree-dweller, this kangaroo's limbs are of equal length, and it also has a long tail and broad feet with non-slip soles.

Interestingly, all kangaroos began as tree-dwellers, but after coming down to the ground one subspecies decided to return to the trees – currently, experts have no idea why. Unlike Skippy and his mates, they are slow and awkward on the ground, moving at little more than walking pace, but they come into their own in the trees, where they can leap as far as 18 m, when making a rapid descent from the tree canopy.

The tree-kangaroo is a solitary creature, apart from in the mating season, and it brings up its young in a pouch, like its hop-along cousin.

CUTEST FEATURE: Its beautiful golden-brown coat
SNUGGLE RATING: ***

LITTLE OWL

Athene noctua

LIVES Hedgerows, woodland and farmland in the UK, Europe, Russia and New Zealand

EATS Small mammals and birds, insects, worms

Unlike many of its nocturnal relatives, this small owl likes to hunt during the day and can often to be seen perching proudly on a fence post or tree stump while scouting for prey. It is a squat little bird with mottled white and greyish-brown feathers and has a very stern, disapproving look about it, due to the dark feathered rings around its large yellow eyes. It has five recognisable calls, including the most common 'kiew' sound, and like many birds it bobs its head up and down when excited or alerted to something. It is a very resourceful bird when it comes to pitching up home, and will happily nest in places as diverse as cliff holes, old buildings and disused rabbit burrows.

The little owl was the messenger of Athena, goddess of wisdom, in Greek mythology and some scholars believe that this is where the idea of the owl being wise derived from. The little owl appears on many Grecian artefacts, including coins, as a sign of protection.

CUTEST FEATURE: Its small, stumpy head

SNUGGLE RATING: ***

CUTE
ANIMAL FACTS

Hamsters have the most extraordinary cheek pouches. Everyone knows that they are like portable larders, where they store food for later, but the mother hamster will also use its pouches to safely transport its tiny young at times of danger!

As every cat owner will testify, cats love to sit on your newspaper when you're trying to read it, but have you considered that perhaps an article might have caught its eye? All those cats with a desire for cat-related mews – sorry – news can now log on to their very own online lifestyle magazine called *Mousebreath.* It contains all the latest catty goings-on in the feline celebrity world, has blogs from literary cats and advice on all the latest moggy accessories! Strictly cats only.

PUFFERFISH

Tetraodontidae (family)
LIVES Tropical and sub-tropical oceans and fresh water
EATS Algae, shellfish

This Christmas-bauble-like fish is among the most unusual-looking of finned sea creatures. A pufferfish can be highly colourful with spots or stripes, or have muted colours to blend in with its environment, though all pufferfish have sharp beaks that enable them to break open shellfish.

Also known as a 'blowfish', it is a weak swimmer, which is a bit of a disadvantage for a fish, but to make up for this it has the amazing ability to ingest vast amounts of water in a very short space of time, to turn itself into an awkward, sometimes spiny, water-filled balloon to deter predators.

Should that not be enough to drive its foe away, it also possesses a lethal and foul-tasting toxin. A dose of this toxic liquid would be enough to kill 30 humans, but surprisingly pufferfish meat is considered a delicacy in Japan, although it must be prepared by a specially trained chef for obvious reasons! The pufferfish ranges in size from a few centimetres in length to around a metre long – quirky, but cute!

CUTEST FEATURE: Its ability to inflate like a balloon!
SNUGGLE RATING: **

CHIPMUNK

Tamias (family)

LIVES North America, northern Asia and Eastern Europe
EATS Nuts, berries, fruits, small insects, birds' eggs

This cute critter looks remarkably similar to its squirrel cousin, with its neat little head and long bushy tail, but it's the dark and light stripes on its face and body which sets it apart, as well as its more diminutive stature.

There are 25 species of chipmunk, and all but one live in North America, the exception being the Asiatic species. It thrives in a variety of habitats, including deserts, mountain ranges, forests and plains, and it likes to live alone in a burrow. Its burrow isn't just your average hole in the ground or log pile nest though, as the chipmunk likes a bit of order and will create at least two rooms: one leaf-lined room for sleeping in, and another for storing food, like a pantry, which is just as well as it hibernates during winter. It has the same ability as a hamster to store and transport food in its bulbous cheek pouches – and this particularly busy nut-smuggler can gather up to 165 acorns a day!

CUTEST FEATURE: Its portable nut store in its stripy cheeks!
SNUGGLE RATING: ***

OPOSSUM

Didelphimorphia (family)
LIVES North America, South America, Patagonia and Argentina
EATS Rats, mice, small birds, reptiles, insects, fruits

This creature is among the rarest of the marsupials: it has a little grey face, pale cheeks and black rings around its eyes, with pale patches on its underside and a grey curly prehensile tail. The opossum will play dead when frightened – an involuntary movement and the reason for the term 'playing possum'. Incredibly, it will not regain consciousness for about an hour.

Despite this unsociable tendency, the opossum is a friendly creature and many have been adopted as pets; one particular opossum in North America has been trained to snowboard! In the wild, the opossum will often live near to human dwellings to make the most of a plentiful supply of rodents, however this little critter has a stomach strong enough to digest even venomous snakes, such as rattlesnakes and vipers. Despite its impressive digestive system, the opossum is of course no match for a human: in Mexico its tail is eaten as an aid to fertility, so it literally has to 'watch its tail'!

CUTEST FEATURE: Its little, pointy face
SNUGGLE RATING: ***

GIRAFFE

Giraffa camelopardalis
LIVES Grasslands and open woodlands in Africa
EATS Fruits, shrubs, twigs, grass

A baby giraffe is 6 ft tall at birth, and has the appearance of being made of elbows, as it's so ungainly and clumsy on its feet! However, it can gallop around within a few hours of being born!

Its horns, which lie flat when it is in the womb, pop up within a day or two. A baby giraffe will remain close to its mother, often standing underneath her so that its mum can give any predators a sharp kick if they come too close. The bond between mum and baby is strong, and it's not until the mother produces another calf that the young giraffe will begin to make its own way in the world.

Between a quarter and a half of baby giraffes reach adulthood in the wild – the reason for this relatively low number is the presence of predators, such as lions and big cats, which will take advantage should they fall over. There are many myths as to how the giraffe grew so tall, including one African belief that it ate too many magic herbs!

CUTEST FEATURE: Its incredibly long limbs
SNUGGLE RATING: ***

GREY SEAL

Halichoerus grypus
LIVES UK and Scillies, Canada, North America, Ukraine
EATS All types of fish, octopuses, crustaceans

This beautiful, white, fluffy, torpedo-shaped pup is a mere 60 cm long when it is born. The pup's mother will feed it for the first two weeks of its life on fat-rich milk, and in that time it can put on around 20 kg of blubber and look almost barrel-shaped, before the mother leaves it to fend for itself.

The pup doesn't resemble a cuddly toy for very long, because within a month it sheds its baby fur and grows a thick grey coat. The grey seal's scientific name translates as 'hook-nose sea-pig', which isn't altogether flattering for such a sweet-faced, placid animal. Its bobbing, inquisitive head is a common sight in UK waters, and its disarming appearance gave rise to the myth of the 'selkie' in the Orkneys, where it is believed that selkie-folk are seals that are transformed into beautiful humans by casting off their skin on reaching the shore.

CUTEST FEATURE: Its silky soft white baby fur and huge eyes
SNUGGLE RATING: ****

SEA TURTLE

Chelonioidea (family)
LIVES Pacific Ocean
EATS Molluscs, crustaceans, fish eggs, seaweed, jellyfish

The baby sea turtle looks almost like a clockwork toy the way it motors along a sandy beach after hatching. It's one of nature's miracles, because as soon as the mother turtle has laid her eggs and buried them on the shore, it is up to the baby turtle, known as a 'hatchling', to do the rest. After between 45 and 70 days of incubation, the little slugger breaks out of its egg and drags itself to the shore where it will wait until the temperature of the sand cools, indicating night-time and a lesser chance of being devoured by predators before making its perilous journey out to sea.

Experts believe that only one in a thousand hatchlings make it to adulthood in the wild – they are very vulnerable and have many predators, including crabs, birds and fish. Once the hatchlings have made it out to sea, it can be ten years before they return to coastal waters, by which time they are up to a metre in diameter! Amazingly, they often return to the very beach where they hatched – it is believed that they are able to navigate their way back by using the earth's magnetic field like a GPS system!

CUTEST FEATURE: The furious flapping it makes to the shoreline
SNUGGLE RATING: ***

CUTE ANIMAL FACTS

Scientists have discovered that there is one animal that has natural rhythm, and the surprising winner of a dance-off in the wild would be a parrot! It can pick up rhythms quickly and stomp and bob its head in time to music or other bird calls.

When is a sheep not a sheep? When it thinks it's a dog! Jack the sheep was adopted as a pet by his owners and brought up with a springer spaniel. Jack has since developed some surprising canine characteristics, including fetching sticks, jumping up on his hind legs, enjoying walkies with his owners, and he even tries to bark and growl! He doesn't recognise that he's a sheep at all and will try to herd a flock of its fellow ovines if placed in a field with them – what must they think?!

CHIMPANZEE

Pan troglodytes
LIVES Forests in Africa
EATS Fruits, leaves, seeds, bark, insects

This forest-dweller is not the quietest of creatures: when it wants to make itself heard by other members of its group – of up to 60 members – it will drum on tree trunks and hoot loudly, which can be heard up to 2 miles away!

The chimp is a companionable fellow; a young individual will remain with its parents for around ten years, learning their habits: how to groom, find food, make nests and tools. Yes, it is great at DIY; for example, it will use long grasses to tease termites out of a mound and use stones as hammers to open nutshells. Chimps will also use stones and sticks as missiles. They are our closest living relative and have been known to live as domestic pets – remember Michael Jackson's chimp, Bubbles? – adopting habits of its human owners, such as drinking tea from a cup and saucer. However, they are not recommended as pets as they need open space and constant stimulation. There are only around 200,000 chimps in the wild and they can live to 50 years of age.

CUTEST FEATURE: Its beautiful, knowing and gentle eyes
SNUGGLE RATING: ★★★★

RUSSIAN DWARF HAMSTER

Phodopus campbelli

LIVES Steppes of Central Asia and mountain regions of China and Russia

EATS Plants, seeds and grains, worms, grubs

Also known as the Campbell's dwarf hamster, having been discovered by W. C. Campbell in 1902 in Tuva (an area that now covers parts of Russia and China), this tiny furball is kept as a pet the world over. The dwarf hamster grows to an average 10 cm, which makes it the perfect furry, pocket-sized companion.

In the wild the hamster will spend much of its time digging large burrows up to 3 ft deep, which it furnishes with grasses and wool, to protect it from predators such as foxes and owls. Unlike other types of hamster, this tiny tot can live in harmony with its fellow furries, and the male hamsters will even act as midwives when the babies come along. Sadly, the Russian dwarf has a short lifespan, living not beyond two years, but if you have one as a pet and give it plenty of things to play with, you can make it the best two years ever!

CUTEST FEATURE: It's super soft and pocket-sized

SNUGGLE RATING: ***

GECKO

Gekotta (family)
LIVES All continents and terrains, apart from Antarctica
EATS Insects, fruits, flower nectar

There are around a thousand varieties of this colourful lizard, which range vastly in size, from the smallest – the Virgin Island gecko, at a few centimetres long – to the largest – the giant day gecko, at around 25 cm long. It has adapted over time to diverse surroundings from tropical rainforests to cold mountainous regions, and to different conditions: for example, the Tokay gecko that lives in eastern Asia has incredible climbing skills, due to tiny hairs on its feet which enable it to climb all manner of vertical surfaces including windows, and the Namib Desert gecko has large webbed feet to enable it to negotiate its way across searing hot sands.

When threatened, the gecko can pull the most extraordinary stunt to escape its foes – if a predator grabs its tail the gecko will shed it, leaving it twitching in its enemy's clutches while it makes its escape! It can also shed its entire skin when threatened. Luckily, the tails and skin both grow back. The tail is a particularly useful piece of kit for the gecko because it helps them balance and it can be used as a fat store for when food is scarce. That's one clever lizard!

CUTEST FEATURE: Its tiny stature and beautiful colours
SNUGGLE RATING: ***

PHOTO CREDITS

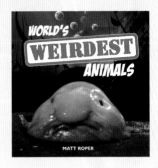

World's Weirdest Animals
Matt Roper

ISBN: 978 1 84024 749 7   Hardback   £6.99

Whales that look like unicorns, lizards that squirt jets of blood from their eyes, naked rats that can sprint backwards... It seems as though some creatures have been put on this earth just to make us laugh.

From the harmless but hilarious to the truly frightening and deadly, the animals in this book are guaranteed to keep you amazed, enthralled and extremely amused.

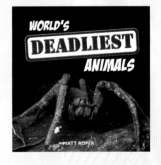

World's Deadliest Animals
Matt Roper

ISBN: 978 1 84953 303 4   Hardback   £6.99

Man-eating maggots, poisonous birds and freshwater fish with teeth as big as a tiger's are just a few of the dangerous and deadly creatures you'll encounter in this book.

From tiny terrors to raging beasts, this collection of the world's deadliest animals contains amazing photographs, gruesome descriptions and shocking stats on real-life monsters of the natural world – proceed with caution!

If you're interested in finding out more about our gift books, follow us on Twitter:
@Summersdale

www.summersdale.com

WORLD'S CUTEST ANIMALS

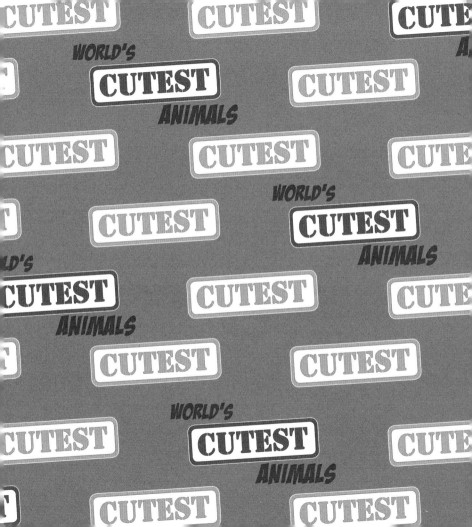